MACPHERSON'S
K-9
COOKBOOK

MACPHERSON'S K-9 COOKBOOK

EASY-TO-MAKE DOG BISCUIT RECIPES

WRITTEN BY MARY MACPHERSON
TASTE-TESTED BY MACDUFF

Sawbuck Ventures Ltd.
Lakefield, Ont.

Canadian Cataloguing in Publication Data

MacPherson, Mary
    MacPherson's K-9 Cookbook: easy-to-
    make dog biscuit recipes

ISBN 0-9682885-0-2

I. Dogs--Food--Recipes.
I. Title. II. Title: K-9 cookbook

SF427.4.M32 1997   636.7'0855

C97-932271-5

Cover design by Woodroe Nicholson
Printed and bound in Canada
Published in Canada by:

    Sawbuck Ventures Ltd.,
    2225 Northey's Rd.,
    RR3 Lakefield, Ont.
    K0L 2H0
    Phone: 705-652-6831

CONTENTS

INTRODUCTION

Baking your own dog biscuits is fun for a lot of reasons. Using *MacPherson's K-9 Biscuit Kit*, you'll be amazed at the satisfaction you'll get from turning out perfectly-shaped biscuits, every time. Best of all, you'll know exactly what ingredients you are feeding your pet. That means several things. You can help keep your dog's diet free of harmful chemicals, additives and preservatives. You can avoid ingredients that don't agree with your dog as a result of health problems associated with aging, such as diabetes and overweight. Also, you can avoid the high cost of commercial dog biscuits, giving your pet a treat it's going to love for just pennies a batch.

The recipes in *MacPherson's K-9 Cookbook* are just a starting point. Don't be afraid to experiment. Use the recipes in this book as a guide. Be creative and add some of your pet's favorite ingredients. On special occasions, be sure and package up some biscuits for a friend's pet. Or better still, give them their own **MacPherson's K-9 Biscuit Kit! Mary**

My name is MacDuff. I am a one-year-old Bedlington Terrier and the official taste-tester of all the recipes in this book. I live with my 12-year-old great aunt, Mickey, who is also a Bedlington Terrier. She helped taste the recipes too, but I'm more finicky so I get to sample the most! (Mickey's a little on the chubby side. I think mom only gives her "Fido's Low Fat Biscuits" and the "Vegetarian Delights", even though she lies in front of the oven when the biscuits are baking. Me, I go outside and stay aloof until I'm called.)

You probably want to know what my favorite biscuit is. I have to tell you, I like them all. But I can make a few personal recommendations. You'll notice one recipe even has my name on it. That's "MacDuff's Peanut Butter Holiday Shortbread". My mom makes these for us as a special treat at Christmas because she knows we love peanut butter and don't get it otherwise.

On the days when I refuse to eat my kibble, I prefer "Bowser's Ranch-Style Beef Bones". I need the protein when I'm trying to get over the backyard fence and round up the neighbor's cows. (And you thought only sheep dogs know how to herd!).

The "Flea Fighter Fingers" have kept me free of fleas all summer—too bad my mom hasn't created a biscuit to repel skunks. Mickey and I both got sprayed this summer!

My teeth are as white as the day I was born, thanks to the "Plaque Buster Biscuits". For everyday treats, you can't beat the "Economy Cookies". And I know my cousins, Maggie and Condor, love the "Holiday Treats" we send them at Christmas. (My mom makes Mickey and I "Holiday Treats" using the large K-9 Cutter, for our birthdays.) Did I mention what a great cook my mom is? She even eats the "Gourmet Food Processor Biscuits" with us!! **MacDuff**

BAKING TIPS

INGREDIENTS

All ingredients in these recipes are available at supermarkets, bulk food stores and health food stores. Always use fresh ingredients. For best results, bring all ingredients to room temperature before starting to bake, unless otherwise indicated.

WORKING WITH YEAST

Three of the recipes call for the use of active, dry yeast. It's sold in bulk, in health food and bulk stores, and also comes in pre-measured packages, containing 2 tsps (10 ml) at supermarkets. Don't be intimidated by this ingredient. It's easy to use. For best results, yeast should be dissolved in warm water between 100°F and 115°F (37.8°C and 46.1°C). Yeast can become stale, so always buy it in small quantities just before baking.

KNEADING THE DOUGH

Kneading the dough thoroughly mixes all the ingredients and makes it smooth and elastic. To knead the dough, turn it out on a clean, well-floured surface. Sprinkle the dough with flour and flour your hands. With the heel of your hands, push the dough away from you, in a quick motion. Then double the dough, pulling the far end of the dough towards you with your fingertips. Turn the dough a quarter turn and repeat the process. Develop a rhythm to your kneading by using your entire body in the action, not just your arms.

ROLLING DOUGH

There is a tendency to roll the dough too thin, perhaps because we are used to rolling pastry and pizza crusts so thin. Be sure and keep the dough between 1/4" and 1/2" in thickness, otherwise the biscuits will be thin and brittle. Keep the rolling surface and the rolling pin well floured at all stages of preparation.

USING THE CUTTERS

Your plastic cutters have been specially designed to cut dog biscuit dough and are made from durable, food-grade plastic. For best results, cut one biscuit at a time and remove it from your floured, rolling surface to the pan before cutting the next biscuit. This way, the dough will not be as likely to stick to the rolling surface. Be sure the cutting edge of the cutter is clean after cutting each biscuit. Cutters are dishwasher friendly.

STORING TIPS

Be sure biscuits are completely cool before storing. The best type of container for room temperature storage is a traditional cookie jar or other type of glass or ceramic jar, with a loose-fitting lid. You can also place your biscuits in an open, cardboard box or an unsealed plastic bag, open to the air. Biscuits stored properly, as noted in each recipe, should keep 3 weeks or more. They may also be refrigerated and frozen. Since your personalized pet biscuits contain no preservatives, be sure to check for mold before serving.

THE RECIPES

ECONOMY COOKIES

Easy and economical to make. A nice, light, beige cookie. Makes about 50 (using small K-9 Cutter).

1/3 cup (75ml) margarine (butter), softened
3 cups (750 ml) whole wheat flour
1/2 cup (125 ml) powdered skim milk
1/4 tsp (1 ml) garlic powder
3/4 cup (175 ml) water, room temperature
1 egg, beaten

1. In a large mixing bowl, cream margarine and flour with a pastry cutter and set aside.
2. In a small bowl, dissolve powdered skim milk and garlic powder in water and whisk in beaten egg.
3. Make a well in the flour mixture and gradually stir in egg mixture until well blended.
4. Knead dough on a floured surface, about 3-4 minutes, until dough sticks together and is easy to work with.
5. With a rolling pin, roll dough to between 1/4" and 1/2" thickness.
6. Cut with K-9 Biscuit Cutter and place on a lightly greased baking sheet.
7. Bake 50 minutes at 325°F (160° C).
8. Cool on a rack until hard and store, at room temperature, in a container with a loose-fitting lid.

MICROWAVE MORSELS

Easy dough to work with. Microwaving makes a chewy treat, ideal for older dogs with missing teeth or difficulty chewing. Makes about 50 (using small K-9 Cutter).

2 chicken bouillon cubes
1 cup (250 ml) boiling water
2 cups (500 ml) whole wheat flour
1/2 cup (125 ml) cornmeal, stone ground
1 1/2 cups (375 ml) powdered skim milk
1 cup (250 ml) quick cooking rolled oats
1/2 cup (125 ml) vegetable oil
2 eggs, beaten

1. In a measuring cup, dissolve bouillon cubes in boiling water and set aside until room temperature.

2. In a large mixing bowl, combine dry ingredients.

3. Make a well in the flour mixture and gradually stir in oil, eggs and bouillon mixture until well blended.

4. Knead dough on a floured surface, about 4-5 minutes, until dough sticks together and is easy to work with.

5. With a rolling pin, roll dough to between 1/4" and 1/2" thickness.

6. Cut with K-9 Biscuit Cutter and place on a micro-proof surface in the microwave.

7. Microwave 5 minutes at medium heat. Carefully turn each biscuit over. Microwave another 5 minutes and turn again. Microwave another 2-5 minutes.

8. Cool on a rack and store in sealed, plastic bags in the refrigerator.

GOURMET FOOD PROCESSOR BISCUITS

Makes a beautiful, flaky, golden biscuit, you'll want to eat with your dog! Makes about 50 (using small K-9 Cutter).

1/4 cup (50 ml) water
2 eggs
2 cups (500 ml) all purpose flour
1 1/3 cups (325 ml) sharp cheddar cheese, shredded
3 cloves garlic, finely chopped
1/2 cup (125 ml) vegetable oil

1. In a small bowl, whisk water and eggs together and set aside.

2. In the bowl of a food processor, equipped with a steel blade, add flour, cheese, garlic and vegetable oil. Pulsate about 5 seconds. Scrape sides of bowl. Pulsate another 5 seconds. Mixture should have the texture of coarse meal.

3. With machine running, drizzle in egg mixture until dough forms a ball.

4. Divide dough into 2 balls, so it is easy to work with.

5. Knead each dough ball on a floured surface, about 3 minutes.

6. With a rolling pin, roll dough to 1/4" thickness.

7. Cut with K-9 Biscuit Cutter and place on a baking sheet, lined with foil.

8. Bake 15 minutes at 400°F (200°C). Remove from oven and carefully turn each biscuit over. Continue baking another 10 minutes.

9. Cool on a rack and store, at room temperature, in a container with a loose-fitting lid.

BREAD MACHINE BISCUITS
(for a 1 1/2-pound loaf machine)

A wonderful, elastic dough that's easy to work with. Makes a dark, golden biscuit with a texture that's medium-hard.
Makes about 40 (using small K-9 Cutter).

1 vegetable bouillon cube
3/4 cup (175 ml) boiling water
1 egg
3 Tbsps (45 ml) vegetable oil
1 cup (250 ml) all purpose flour
1 cup (250 ml) whole wheat flour
1/3 cup (75 ml) bulghur wheat (bulgar)
1/3 cup (75 ml) wheat germ
1/3 cup (75 ml) bran
1/4 cup (50 ml) powdered skim milk
1 tsp (5 ml) garlic powder
1 1/2 tsps (7 ml) active dry yeast

1. In a measuring cup, dissolve bouillon cube in boiling water and set aside until room temperature.
2. Place all the ingredients in the inner pan of a bread machine in the order listed, or in the reverse order, if the manual for your machine specifies dry ingredients first and liquids last.
3. Select the "dough" cycle (or the equivalent for your machine, in some cases the "manual" or "mix bread" setting) and push "start".
4. Prior to "first rise" cycle, remove dough to a floured surface
5. With a rolling pin, roll dough to 1/4" thickness.
6. Cut with K-9 Biscuit Cutter and place on a lightly greased baking sheet.
7. Cover lightly with a tea towel, set in a warm place, and allow to rise 30 minutes.
8. Bake 30 minutes at 325°F (160°C).
9. Cool on a rack and store, at room temperature, in a container with a loose-fitting lid.

PLAQUE BUSTER BISCUITS

This biscuit has a very hard, crunchy texture that will help scrape the build-up of plaque off your dog's teeth. Makes about 70 (using small K-9 Cutter).

3/4 cup (175 ml) powdered skim milk
1/2 cup (125 ml) cornmeal, stone ground
1/4 cup (50 ml) bulghur wheat (bulgar)
2 1/4 cups (550 ml) whole wheat flour
1 chicken bouillon cube
1 1/2 cups (375 ml) boiling water
1 cup (250 ml) quick cooking rolled oats
1 egg, beaten

1. In a mixing bowl, combine powdered skim milk, cornmeal, bulghur wheat and flour and set aside.

2. In a large mixing bowl, dissolve bouillon cube in boiling water. Add rolled oats and let stand, about 5 minutes. Then stir in beaten egg.

3. Gradually stir in dry ingredients, half a cup at a time, until well blended. The last few cupfuls, blend with your hands.

4. Divide dough into 2 balls, so it is easy to work with.

5. Knead each dough ball on a floured surface, about 5 minutes.

6. With a rolling pin, roll dough between 1/4" to 1/2" thickness.

7. Cut with K-9 Biscuit Cutter and place on baking sheet, lined with foil.

8. Bake 50 minutes at 325°F (160°C).

9. Turn oven off and let biscuits cool several hours or overnight, in the oven.

10. Store, at room temperature, in a container with a loose-fitting lid.

FLEA FIGHTER FINGERS

This dough is very easy to handle. It makes a nice, dark biscuit and helps your pet repel fleas because of the presence of brewer's yeast. Makes about 100 (using small K-9 Cutter).

2 beef bouillon cubes
1 3/4 cups (425 ml) boiling water
1 1/2 cups (375 ml) all purpose flour
1 1/2 cups (375 ml) whole wheat flour
1 cup (250 ml) rye flour
1 cup (250 ml) quick cooking rolled oats
1 cup (250 ml) cornmeal, stone ground
1/4 cup (50 ml) brewer's yeast
2 Tbsps (30 ml) garlic powder
1/2 cup (125 ml) vegetable oil
1 egg, beaten

1. In a 2-cup (500 ml) measuring cup, dissolve bouillon cubes in boiling water and set aside until room temperature.
2. In a large mixing bowl, combine dry ingredients.
3. Make a well in the flour mixture and gradually stir in oil, egg and bouillon until well blended.
4. Divide dough into 2 balls, so it is easy to work with.
5. Knead each dough ball on a floured surface, about 3-4 minutes.
6. With a rolling pin, roll dough to between 1/4" and 1/2" thickness.
7. Cut with K-9 Biscuit Cutter and place on a baking sheet, lined with foil.
8. Bake 1 1/2 hours at 300°F (150°F).
9. Cool on a rack until hard and store, at room temperature, in a container with a loose-fitting lid.

BOWSER'S RANCH-STYLE BEEF BONES

Makes a dark, textured, crunchy, meaty-flavored biscuit. Makes about 80 (using small K-9 Cutter).

1 lb (500 g) lean ground beef
2 eggs, beaten
3 cups (750 ml) all purpose flour
1 cup (250 ml) quick cooking rolled oats
1 cup (250 ml) water

1. In a blender or food processor, combine beef and beaten eggs until well blended and set aside.

2. In a large mixing bowl, combine flour and rolled oats. Gradually mix in beef mixture with your hands, until well blended.

3. Add water and stir to form a sticky dough.

4. Divide dough into 2 balls, so it is easy to work with.

5. Knead each dough ball on a well floured surface, about 2 minutes, adding flour until the dough is no longer sticky.

6. With a rolling pin, roll dough to between 1/4" and 1/2" thickness.

7. Cut with K-9 Biscuit Cutter and place on a lightly greased baking sheet.

8. Bake 1 hour at 350°F (180°C).

9. Cool on a rack and store, at room temperature, in a container with a loose-fitting lid.

MICKEY'S COUNTRY COOKIES

A nice elastic dough which makes a dark, well-shaped, crispy biscuit. Makes about 120 (using small K-9 Cutter).

1 pkg (2 tsps (10 ml)) active dry yeast
pinch white sugar
1/4 cup (50 ml) warm water
2 chicken bouillon cubes
1/2 cup (125 ml) powdered skim milk
2 1/4 cups (550 ml) boiling water
1 egg, beaten
1/4 cup (50 ml) honey
1/4 cup (50 ml) vegetable oil
2 cups (500 ml) all purpose flour
4 cups (1 L) whole wheat flour
1 cup (250 ml) wheat germ
1 cup (250 ml) cornmeal, stone ground
2 cups (500 ml) bulghur wheat (bulgar)

1. In a small bowl, dissolve yeast and sugar in warm water and set aside.
2. In a small mixing bowl, dissolve bouillon cubes and powdered skim milk in boiling water and set aside until room temperature. Then whisk in egg,

honey and vegetable oil.

3. In a large mixing bowl, combine flour, wheat germ, cornmeal, and bulghur wheat.

4. Combine yeast mixture and bouillon mixture until well blended.

5. Make a well in the flour mixture and gradually stir in wet ingredients until well blended.

6. Divide dough into 2 balls, so it is easy to work with.

7. Knead each dough ball on a well floured surface, about 4-5 minutes, adding flour until dough is no longer sticky.

8. With a rolling pin, roll dough to 1/2" thickness.

9. Cut with K-9 Biscuit Cutter and place on a lightly greased baking sheet.

10. Cover lightly with a tea towel, set in a warm place, and allow to rise 20 minutes.

11. Bake 20 minutes at 350°F (180°C). Remove from oven and carefully turn each biscuit over. Continue baking another 25 minutes.

12. Cool on a rack and store, at room temperature, in a container with a loose-fitting lid.

SPOT'S GOLDEN CHEESE DREAMS

A nice elastic dough which makes a golden-flecked, chewy treat. Makes about 60 (using small K-9 Cutter).

3 cups (750 ml) whole wheat flour
2 tsps (10 ml) garlic powder
1/2 cup (125 ml) vegetable oil
1 cup (250 ml) shredded cheese
1 egg, beaten
1 cup (250 ml) milk

1. In a large mixing bowl, combine flour and garlic powder.
2. Make a well in the flour mixture and gradually stir in vegetable oil, cheese, beaten egg and milk until well blended.
3. Knead dough on a floured surface, about 3-4 minutes.
4. With a rolling pin, roll dough to 1/2" thickness.
5. Cut with K-9 Biscuit Cutter and place on a lightly greased baking sheet.
6. Bake 25 minutes at 400°F (200°C).
7. Cool on a rack and store, at room temperature, in a container with a loose-fitting lid.

ROADHOUSE MUNCHIES

Makes a nutty-flavored, golden, crunchy biscuit. Makes about 40 (using small K-9 Cutter).

2 cups (500 ml) whole wheat flour
1/2 cup (125 ml) all purpose flour
1/4 cup (50 ml) cornmeal, stone ground
1/2 cup (125 ml) sunflower seeds, shelled
3 eggs
1/4 cup (50 ml) milk
2 Tbsps (30 ml) margarine (butter), softened
1/4 cup (50 ml) molasses

1. In a large mixing bowl, combine flour, cornmeal and sunflower seeds and set aside.

2. In a small bowl, whisk eggs and milk together. Reserve 1 Tbsp (15 ml) of egg mixture in a separate dish for glaze.

3. Make a well in the flour mixture and gradually stir in softened margarine, molasses and egg mixture until well blended.

4. Divide dough into 2 balls, so it is easy to work with.

5. Knead each dough ball on a floured surface, about 2-3 minutes, until dough is no longer sticky.

6. With a rolling pin, roll dough to between 1/4" and 1/2" thickness.

7. Cut with K-9 Biscuit Cutter and place on a baking sheet.

8. With a pastry brush, paint remaining egg mixture on each biscuit.

9. Bake 30 minutes at 350°F (180°C).

10. Turn oven off and let biscuits cool several hours or overnight in the oven.

11. Store, at room temperature, in a container with a loose-fitting lid.

OLD BLUE'S SOFTIES

Ideal for dogs with missing teeth or difficulty chewing. Makes about 140 (using small K-9 Cutter).

1 pkg (2 tsps (10 ml)) active dry yeast
pinch white sugar
1/4 cup (50 ml) warm water
2 chicken bouillon cubes
4 cups (1 L) boiling water
3 1/2 cups (875 ml) all purpose flour
1 1/2 cups (375 ml) whole wheat flour
1 1/2 cups (375 ml) rye flour
1 cup (250 ml) cornmeal, fine ground
1/2 cup (125 ml) powdered skim milk

Glaze:
1 egg
2 Tbsps (30 ml) milk

1. In a small bowl, dissolve yeast and sugar in warm water and set aside.
2. In a medium-sized bowl, dissolve bouillon cubes in boiling water and set aside until room temperature.
3. In a large mixing bowl, combine flour, cornmeal, and powdered skim milk.
4. Combine yeast mixture and bouillon

until well blended.

5. Make a well in the flour mixture and gradually stir wet ingredients into dry until well blended.

6. Divide dough into 2 balls so it is easy to work with.

7. Knead each dough ball on a floured surface, about 1 minute.

8. With a rolling pin, roll dough to between 1/4" and 1/2" thickness.

9. Cut with K-9 Biscuit Cutter and place on a baking sheet, sprayed with a no-stick cooking spray.

10. In a small bowl, whisk egg and milk to make a glaze.

11. With a pastry brush, paint each biscuit with egg mixture.

12. Bake 25 minutes at 300°F (150°C). Remove from oven and carefully turn each biscuit over. Continue baking another 25 minutes.

13. Cool on rack and store in sealed, plastic bags in the refrigerator.

14. If biscuits become hard with prolonged storage, place each biscuit in the microwave for 5-10 seconds on high. Cool to room temperature before serving.

SNIFF N' BITE BISCUITS

A nice, light-colored, firm, aromatic biscuit. Makes 50 (using small K-9 Cutter).

2 1/2 cups (625 ml) whole wheat flour
1/2 cup (125 ml) powdered skim milk
1 Tbsp (15 ml) brown sugar
2 tsps (10 ml) garlic powder
1/4 cup (50 ml) margarine (butter), softened
1 egg, beaten
1/2 cup (125 ml) plus 2 Tbsps (30 ml) ice water

1. In a large mixing bowl, combine flour, powdered skim milk, sugar and garlic powder.

2. With a pastry cutter, blend in margarine.

3. Make a well in the flour mixture and gradually stir in egg and ice water until well blended. Use hands at the end to form a ball.

4. Divide dough into 2 balls, so it is easy to work with.

5. Knead each dough ball on a floured surface, about 2 minutes.

6. With a rolling pin, roll dough to between 1/4" and 1/2" thickness.

7. Cut with K-9 Biscuit Cutter and place on a baking sheet, lined with foil.

8. Bake 30 minutes at 350°F (180°C).

9. Cool on a rack and store, at room temperature, in a container with a loose-fitting lid.

OVER THE RAINBOW TREATS

An easy dough to work with. Makes a nice firm, speckled biscuit. Makes about 55 (using small K-9 Cutter).

1 cup (250 ml) canned mixed peas and carrots, drained
2 1/2 cups (625 ml) whole wheat flour
1/2 cup (125 ml) powdered skim milk
1 tsp (5 ml) garlic powder
6 Tbsps (90 ml) vegetable oil
1 egg, beaten
1/2 cup (125 ml) ice water

1. In a blender or a food processor purée carrots and peas and set aside.
2. In a large mixing bowl, combine flour, powdered skim milk, and garlic powder.
3. Make a well in the flour mixture and gradually stir in puréed vegetables, oil, beaten egg and ice water until well blended.
4. Divide dough into 2 balls, so it is easy to work with.
5. Knead each dough ball on a floured surface, about 2 minutes.
6. With a rolling pin, roll dough to between 1/4" and 1/2" thickness.
7. Cut with K-9 Biscuit Cutter and place on a baking sheet, lined with foil.
8. Bake 15 minutes at 350°F (180°C). Remove from oven and carefully turn each biscuit over. Continue baking another 25 minutes.
9. Cool on a rack and store, at room temperature, in a container with a loose-fitting lid

FIDO'S LOW FAT BISCUITS

A stiff dough that makes a toastie-brown, crunchy treat. Makes about 50 (using small K-9 Cutter).

2 cups (500 ml) whole wheat flour
1/2 cup (125 ml) all purpose flour
1/4 cup (50 ml) cornmeal, stone ground
1/4 cup (50 ml) quick cooking rolled oats
1 1/2 tsps (7 ml) garlic powder
2 Tbsps (30 ml) vegetable oil
2 egg whites
1/4 cup (50 ml) molasses
1/4 cup (50 ml) skim milk
2 Tbsps (30 ml) cold water

1. In a large mixing bowl, combine flour, cornmeal, rolled oats and garlic powder.
2. In a small bowl, whisk oil, egg whites, molasses, milk and water.
3. Make a well in the flour mixture and gradually stir in egg mixture until well blended.
4. Divide dough into 2 balls, so it is easy to work with.
5. Knead each dough ball on a well floured surface, about 2 minutes.
6. With a rolling pin, roll dough to 1/2" thickness.
7. Cut with K-9 Biscuit Cutter and place on a baking sheet, lined with foil.
8. Bake 30 minutes at 350°F (180°C). Turn oven off and leave biscuits to harden for 1 hour.
9. Cool on a rack and store, at room temperature, in a container with a loose-fitting lid.

VEGETARIAN DELIGHTS

Makes a beautifully formed, crisp, tan-colored biscuit. Makes about 95 (using small K-9 Cutter).

1 cup (250 ml) quick cooking rolled oats
1/4 cup (50 ml) margarine (butter) softened
1 1/2 cups (375 ml) hot water
2 cloves garlic, crushed
1 Tbsp (15 ml) butter
1/2 cup (125 ml) powdered skim milk
1 egg, beaten
1 cup (250 ml) cornmeal, stone ground
1 cup (250 ml) wheat germ
2 1/2 cups (625 ml) whole wheat flour
1/2 cup (125 ml) rye flour

Wash:
2 Tbsps (30 ml) milk

1. In a large mixing bowl, combine rolled oats, margarine and hot water and let stand 5 minutes.
2. In a frying pan, sauté garlic in butter.
3. Add garlic, powdered skim milk, and beaten egg to rolled oats mixture, stirring until well blended.
4. In a bowl, combine cornmeal, wheat germ and flour.
5. Gradually add flour mixture, half a cup at a time, until well blended.
6. Knead dough on a floured surface, about 3-4 minutes.
7. With a rolling pin, roll dough to 1/2" thickness.
8. Cut with K-9 Biscuit Cutter and place on a baking sheet, lined with foil.
9. With a pastry brush, coat each biscuit lightly with milk.
10. Bake 1 hour at 300°F (150°C).
11. Turn oven off and leave biscuits in oven until cool.
12. Store, at room temperature, in a container with a loose-fitting lid.

MACDUFF'S PEANUT BUTTER HOLIDAY SHORTBREAD

Dough is a little tricky to work with at first, but makes a perfectly formed, golden doggie shortbread. Makes about 55 (using small K-9 Cutter).

1 1/2 cups (375 ml) whole wheat flour
1/2 cup (125 ml) all purpose flour
1 Tbsp (15 ml) baking powder
1 cup (250 ml) peanut butter (smooth or chunky)
3/4 cup (175 ml) milk

1. In a large mixing bowl, combine flour and baking powder.
2. In a small bowl, whisk peanut butter and milk until smooth.
3. Make a well in the flour mixture and gradually stir in peanut butter mixture until well blended.
4. Use hands to work dough into 2 pliable balls. The warmth from your hands will help make the dough more workable.
5. Knead each dough ball on a floured surface, about 2 minutes.
6. With a rolling pin, roll dough between 1/4" and 1/2" thickness.
7. Cut with K-9 Biscuit Cutter and place on a baking sheet, lined with foil.
8. Bake 15 minutes at 400°F (200°C).
9. Cool on a rack and store in sealed, plastic bags in the refrigerator.

HOLIDAY TREATS

This is a stiff dough to work with, but makes picture-perfect, dark, golden biscuits. The large batch is ideal for holiday gift giving. Makes 140 (using the small K-9 Cutter).

1 pkg (2 tsps (10 ml)) active dry yeast
pinch sugar
1/4 cup (50 ml) warm water
2 beef bouillon cubes
2 cups (500 ml) boiling water
1/4 cup (50 ml) milk
1/4 cup (50 ml) + 3 Tbsps (45 ml) honey
1 egg, beaten
1/4 cup (50 ml) vegetable oil
2 1/2 cups (625 ml) all purpose flour
3 cups (750 ml) whole wheat flour
1 cup (250 ml) cornmeal, stone ground
1 cup (250 ml) wheat germ
2 cups (500 ml) bulghur wheat (bulgar)
3/4 cup (175 ml) wheat bran
3/4 cup (175 ml) quick cooking rolled oats
3/4 cup (175 ml) cheddar cheese
Glaze:
1/2 beef bouillon cube
pinch garlic powder
1/4 cup (50 ml) boiling water
1 Tbsp (15 ml) vegetable oil

1. In a small bowl, dissolve yeast and sugar in warm water and set aside.

2. In a small mixing bowl, dissolve bouillon cubes in boiling water and set aside until room temperature. Then whisk in milk, honey, beaten egg and vegetable oil.

3. In a large mixing bowl, combine flour, cornmeal, wheat germ, bulghur wheat, wheat bran, rolled oats and cheese.

4. Whisk yeast and first bouillon mixture until well blended.

5. Make a well in the flour mixture and gradually stir in wet ingredients, until well blended.

6. Divide dough into 3 balls, so it is easy to work with.

7. Knead each dough ball on a well floured surface, about 3-4 minutes.

8. With a rolling pin, roll dough to 1/2" thickness.

9. Cut dough with K-9 Biscuit Cutter and place on a baking sheet sprayed with a no-stick cooking spray.

10. Cover lightly with a tea towel, set in a warm place, and let rise 30 minutes.

11. Bake 20 minutes at 350°F (180°C). Remove from oven and carefully turn each biscuit over. Continue baking another 25 minutes.

12. In a measuring cup, dissolve 1/2 bouillon cube and garlic powder in boiling water and whisk in oil.

13. With a pastry brush, paint tops of biscuits with bouillon mixture.

14. Turn oven off and return biscuits to oven. Let biscuits remain in oven until cool.

15. Store, at room temperature, in a container with a loose-fitting lid.

NOTES:

NOTES: